# A TRIP TO THE
# POST OFFICE

Josie Keogh

**PowerKiDS** press.

New York

Published in 2013 by The Rosen Publishing Group, Inc.
29 East 21st Street, New York, NY 10010

First Edition

Editor: Amelie von Zumbusch
Book Design: Ashley Drago

Photo Credits: Cover © www.iStockphoto.com/Kim Gunkel; p. 5 iStockphoto/Thinkstock; p. 6 Joe Raedle/Getty Images News/Getty Images; pp. 9, 22, 24 Shutterstock.com; p. 10 Jeff Topping/Getty Images News/Getty Images; p.13 Leanne Temme/Photolibrary/Getty Images; p. 14 © www.iStockphoto.com/Mark Bowden; p. 17 © www.iStockphoto.com/Claude Dagenais; p. 18 Jupiterimages/Pixland/Thinkstock; p. 21 Photo Researchers/Getty Images.

Library of Congress Cataloging-in-Publication Data

Keogh, Josie.
 A trip to the post office / by Josie Keogh. — 1st ed.
    p. cm. — (Powerkids readers: my community)
 Includes index.
 ISBN 978-1-4488-7404-0 (library binding) — ISBN 978-1-4488-7483-5 (pbk.) —
ISBN 978-1-4488-7557-3 (6-pack)
 1. Postal service—Juvenile literature. I. Title.
 HE6078.K46 2013
 383'.42—dc23
                                    2011049397

Manufactured in the United States of America

CPSIA Compliance Information: Batch #CS12PK: For Further Information contact Rosen Publishing, New York, New York at 1-800-237-9932

# CONTENTS

The post office is on Main Street.

It is busy.

7

Trucks bring mail.

The mail comes in big bags.

Jen sends a card.

13

It is to her dad.

15

Jim checks his PO box.

18

He got a package!

Dee buys a stamp. It is for her note.

2002

22

Sam buys stamps. She collects stamps.

# WORDS TO KNOW

**counter**: A place where people do business.

**envelope**: A paper covering.

**mailbox**: A box people put mail in.

## INDEX

## WEBSITES

Due to the changing nature of Internet links, PowerKids Press has developed an online list of websites related to the subject of this book. This site is updated regularly. Please use this link to access the list:
www.powerkidslinks.com/pkrc/post/